John Brown

The Days

Julian Ashbourn

This book is dedicated to my dear wife Joanna, whose secret garden of love has nurtured many plants and animals who have been fortunate enough to find it, including the man who humbly writes these words.

Contents

Introduction

This book is highly unusual, in both its structure and content. Some may find it difficult to comprehend at an intellectual level. Indeed, I struggle with it myself. I know not from where it came, or why it was necessary to put it into words, but I did feel a compelling urge to write it. It might have adopted many guises and it may yet reflect a different set of values and perspectives, depending upon the readers own point of view.

My hope is that it will take the reader on a journey. Perhaps, into the unknown, but certainly upon a voyage of discovery of one sort or another. Maybe this journey will be self-revealing, maybe it will be enlightening upon a broader level. Maybe the reader will lose their bearings entirely and wander through, as if in a desert land. But perhaps, even so, they will stumble upon an oasis, with water so clear and pure. that it will suddenly reflect everything. Perhaps the book will have a very special, personal meaning to the reader, or perhaps no meaning at all. Just ink on paper. It is impossible to foretell the impact that this book may have upon the reader. In any event, I do hope that it provides an opportunity to reflect upon that which is truly important in life, and to be able to identify and discriminate against that which is of mere superficial value. Also, to be able to place things within a broader perspective. To nurture a broader understanding.

In our modern world, we tend to become absorbed by the fast moving furore around us and spend so little time thinking and reflecting. Some attempt to escape by meditation, but this provides few, if any answers. Some look back to ancient times, but find only a limited vista with which to engage. The answers, if they exist, are surely already within us. They have been accumulating over millions of years and countless generations. We just need the key to unlock a particular train of thought that will remove the veil and let us see things within a true context of humanity. Perhaps the reader will find a key within the pages of this book. I do hope so.

J.A.

1. First Days

How beautiful was our early world. Great golden plains stretched out as far as the eye could see, cosseted by big skies of azure blue, blending into gold as they kissed the sun. Up in the mountains, the majestic peaks of granite and limestone, wore their crowns of pure white snow and caused sparkling streams of pure, life giving water, to flow down gently, twisting and turning, until they reached the green valleys below. Out on the very edges of the land. great coastal waves came and crashed against the rocks, to make their own special music and swathes of gold and silver sands stretched out for miles, unsullied by any human foot. In the great forests, another world existed. A world teeming with life as every creation depended upon every other creation, each with its special place within the greater tapestry of life. And, deep in the oceans, yet another world, wrapped within a quiet, gentle aura of the deep and yet, playing out its own beautifully choreographed stories, as they had been enacted a thousand times before. All of this, and more, existing upon our beautiful blue planet as it swirled its way through space and time, somewhere within that greater ballet of the universe, within which, space and time themselves are inscrutable. We are not given the understanding of the stars, but may simply admire and wonder.

We place our own, rudimentary measure upon that which we perceive as time. We have created an arbitrary dissection of years, months, weeks, days, hours, minutes and seconds, which helps us to place events into some sort of context, at least within our own understanding. Following this tradition, I am writing this work at the start of the year 2018. That is, two thousand and eighteen years into what we call the Christian era, named after the prophet Jesus Christ. Of course, there were other prophets before and after Christ and humans existed long before this date, as we know from the ancient civilisations, notably the Egyptians and Chinese. And so, we must stretch our system of measurement to reflect a time before Christ (BC) and, for geological time, much further. Within the context of civilised human life, it makes little difference where or when we place our character, John Brown, for his is a story which could apply at any time and within any culture. Indeed,

John Brown is simply a symbol of humanity. At a different point of time, his circumstances may have been different and his influences of a different hue. However, the important facets of his life, as a human being, would have been similar.

John Brown came into this world on January 24th 1948 at the London Hospital on the Whitechapel Road, in what is known as the East End of London. His parents, Arthur and Elsie, lived in a small rented, terraced house at number 16 John Street, off of Sutton Street East, which was itself off of the Commercial Road, also in the East End. Arthur had been a soldier during the war and was extremely lucky to land a job in the badly bomb damaged docklands area, at a small engineering firm, named Hartland Engineering, on Pennington Street, just north of the main London dock at Wapping. It was no doubt the fact that Arthur had been in the Royal Engineers that secured him the job, although his duties at Hartland's were very different from what he experienced during the war. Now, he stood at a lathe all day long, turning out gear wheels, whose purpose and final destination he never did discover. Still, he was glad of the job as he well understood the difficulties that returning servicemen had faced at the end of hostilities, especially in London. Elsie was also a Londoner, born in Crediton Hill, in West Hampstead, to a family that was decimated by the war, with all of her three brothers and one sister lost. Like Arthur, her view of the world had been shattered by the war, although, coming from simple families, neither of them really understood this. Like many millions of others, they were glad to see the coming of peacetime, but also felt hollow inside, as though something was missing. Something precious had gone and would never return, no matter how hard they pretended otherwise.

And so, this was the world that John Brown entered. Named simply after the street in which his parents lived, he spent a short time in the London Hospital and was then returned to John Street, where he spent most of his young life lying in a makeshift cot in the upstairs bedroom. From time to to time, some neighbour or other would come and peer into his little box and make funny, incomprehensible noises, to which John responded the best he could under the circumstances. His view of the outside world was constrained by the geometry of the little room in which he was placed. He was very rarely moved or taken outside, although 16 John Street did have a small back yard. It could not be called a garden, as nothing grew there, but at least it offered a view of the sky and the occasional passing bird. But his were not loving parents. They simply regarded the baby as another entity which had to be dealt with, along with all their other tasks, trials and tribulations. Another drain upon their already limited finances. Elsie had aspirations to take in sewing and washing in order to boost their income, but everyone in the area was in a similar position to themselves and this idea, like others of Elsie's, soon petered out into nothing. Such was the Brown household at this time, incremented as it was by baby John.

Things might have been very different. Fate might have decreed that John be born into a wealthy family with a beautiful country mansion. There, he would have been pampered from birth, swathed in comfortable attire and adored by everyone around him. More importantly, he would have been engaged intellectually, with his parents keen to get him to talk as soon as possible and constantly showing him interesting things. He would, as his days passed, be introduced to an unending stream of similarly interesting people, all of whom would seem delighted to make his acquaintance and would engage directly with him. When not being attended to by his nanny, he would be in the loving arms of his mother, enjoying her reassuring voice and feeling a strong sense of belonging. His every waking moment would be a new adventure in this exciting world into which he had been born and in which his future was assured.

Or perhaps he might have been born thousands of years ago in ancient Egypt, into a family of well connected artisans. His mother would have doted on him, wrapping him in fine linen and eager to show him to all her relatives and neighbours. He would soon come to know the warmth of the sun and the scents and sounds which wafted through that fertile valley, carried on the breeze, like so many interesting things to contemplate as he lay in his cot. There would always be people around. Family members would come and talk to him, elder sisters would come and kiss him on the forehead and make soothing sounds and, from time to time, his adoring mother would come and take him in her arms to feed him, before rocking him slowly to sleep, wrapped securely in her love. Sometimes, his father would hold him and encourage him to repeat the sounds that he was making, ensuring that the infant would soon be talking. In the background, enquiries would be made as to the boys future and, it might be decided, that he would be properly trained as a scribe, just as soon as he reached the appropriate age. In the meantime, he would be adored by the whole family, given pet names and exposed to a world of sunshine and happiness.

Perhaps he might have been borne into a nomad Bedouin tribe a couple of hundred years ago where, as a boy, he would have received strict training in both practical and honourable matters. He would have been pampered and given much more attention than his sisters, if he had any. As soon as he could walk and talk, he would have been proudly introduced to all relatives, who would no doubt shower him with little gifts and show great admiration of him as a future potential leader. The roaming lifestyle would be all that he knew and it would seem strange to him that people settled into towns and did not seem to go anywhere in particular. He would have a great appreciation of food and, especially, water, understanding its value in the world in which he lived. Despite the nomadic life of his family, he would be dressed in fine robes and would soon come to appreciate valuable metals and gemstones, developing a refined aesthetic appreciation which he would never lose.

Or he might have been born an Indian Prince, a few hundred years ago, when the ancient civilisations blended into the new. He would have been surrounded by luxury at every turn and his wishes would have been immediately answered by a team of servants, whose sole task would be to look after him. As soon as he could walk, he would have been paraded in front of visiting nobles and would be in no doubt as to his superior station in life. Everyone would dote on him and he could have, more or less, whatever he wanted. He would have slept on huge silk pillows and worn the finest silk robes, of many colours. He would have been indoctrinated into the religious traditions of his family and taught that theirs was the only true religion. He would start his religious and academic education at an early age, being surrounded by tutors, holy men and advisors. Right from the start, he would view women as subservient to men and expect them to wait on him accordingly. Later, this attitude would become less benign.

Maybe he would be born into a poor Filipino family in the 20th century. One of many children, he would be surrounded by noise and clutter, with his mother doing her best to cope with living in a shanty town among hundreds of others, all living a hand to mouth existence. His father might be a fisherman, very dependent upon local seasonal conditions. Sometimes they would have everything they needed. Sometimes they might go hungry. His fate might be to follow a similar path, perpetuating the conditions under which he, himself was born. But he would have no inkling of that as an infant, He would simply play with whatever he found to play with and learn, mostly by example, from his brothers and sisters. His mother would have a natural love for her infants, but would have little idea of how to translate this into a practical upbringing for them.

Or perhaps he would be born into mid 20th century America, thrust into a materialistic society where everything depended upon perception and wealth. His parents would show some fascination with him as an early infant, but they would be thinking ahead as to what he will eventually do for the family name and hoping that he would be successful later in life. They would buy him toys and expect him to play with them, but there would be little in the way of natural, parental love and attention. Even as a small toddler he would reflect the grasping nature of life around him, holding his toys to himself and wanting everything he sees. This would be seen as humorous by his parents who, no doubt, would encourage such behaviour. His contact outside the family would be little, except for with visiting relatives, and so his perspective on the strange world around him would also have been rather limited.

Yes, John could have been born anywhere, at any time and into any culture, but fate decreed that his entry into life would be via the London Hospital, on a cold, bleak day in January 1948, before being taken down to John Street and installed in the back bedroom, with a single little window overlooking a dismal back yard. This was his first experience of life, which he shared mostly with his working class parents, Arthur and Elsie. He was a little under-nourished, as many post war working class children were in England, but otherwise in reasonable health physically. However, he was sadly neglected from an emotional point of view, receiving neither love nor guidance of any kind from his parents. As a toddler, he simply existed from day to day. He had no idea who he was or why he was there, or the purpose of anything that went on around him. He was never inspired or taught to see the magic in anything. As soon as he could feel, he felt the hollow ache of loneliness, although he didn't know that this was what it was, or why he was feeling it. Consequently, he increasingly saw the world as two worlds. The private world that he inhabited and the other world where everybody else went about their business. Actually, he never felt a part of that other world and this early experience would mark him for life. In truth, he never would feel a part of that other world, where everybody else existed. It just went on around him as he caught occasional glimpses of it from his own world.

Perhaps John's first days were similar to the first days of other children born into that awkward era of post war Britain and, indeed elsewhere. But they were nevertheless a minority. They would never quite fit into a world populated by other children who were more self-assured, more confident, more loved and, therefore, more successful. The situation would not have been dissimilar in other ages. The emotional neglect of children is a terrible thing and is, in fact, a crime against humanity, if you perceive humanity in the deeper sense.

2. School Days

John had no idea what a school was. He first started to hear the word when he was around four years of age. It was always mentioned in a derogatory manner, as if it was some horrible place where bad children were sent. From about four and a half years, his mother often stated that she would be glad when he went to school and she could see the back of him. His father simply did not comment and seemed to take no interest at all in the matter. As a result of this cruel conditioning, John began to dread the very thought of school, convinced that it was something to be feared. As the day of his starting school approached, he became increasingly apprehensive about the whole idea although, naturally, he could not discuss this with anyone. He was equipped with some plastic sandals and a tatty cardigan and, on the day, packed off to join a line of other children walking to the St Anne's primary school, a few streets away. He did not know who any of the other five year olds were, but noted that most of them had their mother with them on this important first day at school, whereas he did not. He trudged along in silence and, as he went, with his gaze turned towards the wet pavement, he noticed that he was also the only one wearing plastic sandals, while most of the others had proper lace-up leather shoes, except for some of the girls who had slip-on shoes over white socks. He was already feeling different from the other children, and somewhat inferior. He tagged along behind a small group who were accompanied by two mothers, each of whom was smiling and saying kind, encouraging words to their young children. He wished that one of them was his mother.

As they turned into Cannon Street and walked north, John could see a large, square looking building up ahead, which already had children milling about noisily in the road outside, as they took their leave of their loving parent. As he had no such loving parent in tow, he simply stayed with his adopted group and followed them along the path and, having said their goodbyes, up to a set of wide opening wooden panelled doors with a wide brass handle on each. There was quite a lot of noise coming from the inside, as excited children learned which classes they had been assigned to and chattered away among themselves as they went to and fro. This was something that John was unaccustomed to and he was already feeling rather frightened and bewildered by the whole experience. He wandered in and remained in the main hallway with its half height painted green and cream walls, separated by a thin black horizontal line, looking not dissimilar to a prison, although John, thankfully, hadn't seen one of those. As he stood there, not knowing quite what to do, the mass of children slowly dispersed and he became increasingly exposed. Eventually, an austere looking lady, dressed head to foot in grey, approached him and demanded, in a sharp voice, to know his name. John whispered his name, only to be commanded to say it louder, upon compliance with which, the stern lady looked him up in her papers attached to a clipboard. She blurted out something that sounded like 'three bee' and, taking John by the arm, hurried off down the hallway. On either side of the hallway were occasional blocks of windows, adjoining wide, dark wooden doors which themselves were half glazed. Pushing one of these doors open, the lady in grey pushed John inside before disappearing again down the hallway. Inside, another lady peered over her spectacles at John, as though he were some sort of specimen, and then ordered him to find a desk and sit down. John could see around twenty or so other children sitting at desks and, upon spying an empty desk towards the rear of the class, made his way towards it. As he did so, every other child in the class stared at him, some of them giggling, but all of them wearing expressions which seemed far from friendly. John felt close to tears as he ran the gauntlet of the other children until, finally, reaching the desk and sitting down, next to another boy who stared at him intently.

There were some blank exercise books and pencils on each desk and the morning was spent copying letters from the blackboard, after being instructed, very firmly, by the teacher to do so. But John had never done anything like this before. No-one at home had ever even mentioned writing to him, let alone taught him to read and write. As a consequence, he had no idea what he was doing or why he was doing it. Not surprisingly, his copied letters were quite bad. Completely out of proportion with one another and poorly resembling the examples on the board. When the teacher finally came around to examine his work, she was furious and shouted at him, as though he had done something terrible. John couldn't understand and sat in silence, the tears rolling down his cheeks. After the teacher had returned, in obvious frustration, to her own desk, the boy sitting next to John, whose name was Graham, asked him if he hadn't done writing before. John had never even heard the word. Graham explained it to him as best he could and John endeavoured to try harder. However, John's incompetence at copying letters and learning to read and write, was excelled by his incompetence at figures. Once again, they were completely unfamiliar to him. His parents had never explained to him what mathematics, or arithmetic as it was known in primary school, was. To John, it was simply a collection of strange symbols, arranged in a particular manner, from which, as if by magic, you were supposed to deduce a further line of strange symbols. He had no idea of the fundamental purpose of arithmetic. After a while, he began to learn by rote at least some of the answers, but there was a limit to how much could be stashed into his young memory. He frustrated teacher after teacher with his inability to grasp the fundamentals, simply because nobody took the trouble to sit down with him and explain the purpose of what he was doing. His parents were no help at all in this context and there were no books at home that he could learn from. John simply did not understand what education was really for and why it was necessary for him to go through all the exercises that he was faced with at school.

The first few years at school were, for John Brown, something of a nightmare, although, he found that he was quite interested in history and, to some degree, art. He liked subjects based around humanity, but could never get enthusiastic about mathematics or the sciences. This was not a failing on the part of John Brown, but a tragic failure of the in place system, to teach, motivate and inspire young pupils in these all important subjects. Furthermore, the system compounded the error by categorising all such children as John, as backward or lazy, which was simply not the case. Had he had loving, interested parents, they would have spotted this error and taken steps to correct it, but, alas, this was not the case either. And so John Brown meandered his way through primary school until it was time to take the 11 plus examination, which would determine his fate as far as secondary schools were concerned. Those who passed the 11 plus exam would be offered a place at a grammar school. Those who failed the exam would be relegated back to a comprehensive school which, in reality, was a dumping ground for children who were not destined for any kind of professional life. They would be put through the motions of teaching, but no-one really had any expectations for them and nobody really cared.

John Brown took the exam and had no difficulty answering almost all of the questions. Indeed, he was feeling quite proud of himself at the end of the two hour ordeal and was confident that he would surely pass. After all, he was, by now, getting quite interested in the concept of education and was, in fact, showing promise in several subjects. When the results were announced, only a small number of children had passed the 11 plus exam at John's school. Many were shocked and thought that there must have been something wrong. There was. The reality was that there were only a certain number of grammar school places available and they tended to go to pupils of the preferred schools, of which John's was not one. Consequently, a great many young pupils were dealt a bitter blow, both to their own self confidence and to their belief in their country. They had, effectively, been dismissed as second class citizens in whom the system had little interest. Some would have the necessary spirit and will to overcome this disadvantage, but most would not. They would simply drift through their secondary school education, as they had done at the primary school. John Brown was one such student. Furthermore, some of these schools didn't have the facility to offer the formal qualifications of the day, resulting in large numbers of perfectly capable youngsters leaving school without a single qualification to their name, usually at the age of 14 or 15. It was assumed that these individuals would make up the ranks of the working class. John Brown would bolster their number by one.

Of course, it might have all been so very different. If John had been born into a well to do, wealthy family a decade or so earlier, his schooling would all have planned, in meticulous detail, before he could even walk. Prior to starting school, his parents would have engaged him in many intellectual pursuits, reading books with him and explaining in detail anything in which he showed an interest. They would have ensured that he could read, write and undertake basic arithmetic before going to school. The schools that he was to attend would have been chosen very carefully in advance and, in all likelihood, he would have been interviewed by the headmaster of each school before attending, in order to understand precisely the environment in which he was to become a part. He would have sat for regular examinations, all of which he would have sailed through without difficulty, amassing a string of qualifications before leaving age. After secondary school, he would have gone to one of the universities or, perhaps entered military training. In any event his future would be assured. Furthermore, he would proceed along this path with confidence, knowing exactly why he was doing so and what he would become in later life.

Had he been born into a well established bedouin family before the turn of the twentieth century, he may not have received an academic education in the sense that a European would understand, but he would have been nonetheless well trained, from infancy, in the customs of his people. He would be taught how to ride horses and camels, would have been literate and numerate and would have had a solid appreciation of the history of his people, including the various other tribes in the desert. He would also have had an aesthetic appreciation and would learn to value quality in all things. Accordingly, he would also learn the necessary skills of bartering and would become shrewd in his dealings with others. If he had sisters, they would be less fortunate however, as his would be a male centred world.

Other cultures would maintain a dichotomy between the better and less well educated, with education often being a mark of privileged families. Whether one was born into such a family or not was a matter of chance. In ancient China, one might have been born into a world of beautiful things, wherein the individual would also have been extremely well educated, especially if male. An uneducated family may have been tradespeople of various standing, some wealthy, some less so and, of course, there would be those who lived in poverty. The same might be said of India, where extremely wealthy families walked on the same paths as those suffering from hunger and disease. The well to do families would send their children to England or France in order to receive an education, indeed, they still continue the practice. Those who were less well born would receive no formal education at all.

However, in most cultures, at most times, the path of education would have been reasonably clear. There were those who would simply have no expectation at all of receiving any formal education. They would simply pick up the rudimentary skills, as required for their everyday existence, from their own families. Literacy may or may not be included in this list of skills. Those who were more fortunate and found themselves born into substantial families, would attend good quality formal schools, either in their own country or overseas, depending upon the standing and influence of the family. The children involved would understand this and feel that it was their right to be so educated, thus maintaining a class distinction which is the basis of so many cultures, whether acknowledged or otherwise.

But at least these paths and positions were clear. John Brown and many other children in post war Britain, had a much less clear situation to deal with. On the one hand, their's was, or had been, a successful country who had given so much to the world in terms of civilisation, science and the arts and was still regarded as a world power. On the other hand, the privileged positions and advantages that many associated with the country were only available to a particular section of society. The class system remained very much in force and does so to this day. The awful thing was the pretence. The pretence that John Brown was born into a classless system of equal opportunity. The reality was that he was born into a sort of no mans land where, had he been loved and properly guided by his parents, he may have found his way out of it, Without this support however, he was doomed to wander in obscurity throughout these critical days which would serve to shape his entire life. If the days had been positive and filled with proper guidance and achievement, he would have had a professional career path mapped out ahead of him. But they were not. They were instead filled with neglect, poor tuition and a general lack of interest from those around him, which all served to condemn John Brown to a life of mediocrity, even before he had attended his first day at school.

3. Teenage Days

Out of school and out of work, with his parents continuingly nagging him to get a job and stop sponging off of them for his existence, John Brown's latter teenage days were a misery. He still saw no purpose to his life, at least, as far as it had proceeded thus far. Upon leaving school, a careers advisor had advised of only one position, that of a delivery boy at the local butcher's shop. John might have taken up the position except that, when he arrived for an interview with the butcher, he was told that the position was filled. He fell into a cycle of doing whatever odd jobs he could while he looked for steady work. Arthur and Elsie Brown had convinced themselves that their only son was lazy and simply did not want to work. Thus, every evening, he was met with a barrage of insults and ensuing argument. Arthur had forgotten how lucky he was to get a job after the war, while many of his fellow servicemen had found it very hard indeed, some of them not working for years, some of them emigrating and some becoming so disillusioned that they even considered suicide, except that that was an offence in the brave new world in which they now found themselves. The uneducated masses just took whatever work they could get in order to survive and, those who could not find work, would have to be supported by their friends or relatives.

This was the world in which a teenage John Brown found himself. Somewhere, in the back of his mind, was an idea that life should be better than this. In his daydreams, he dreamed of himself being a successful professional person and, like many teenagers, he dreamed of being in love. He imagined what it would be like to have a decent and kind young lady falling in love with him and how happy they would be together. In his dreams, he would do anything for his beloved. He would live and breath just for her and would walk through fire for her if it were to become necessary to do so. He dreamed of holding her in his arms, and how he would be her protector and love her with all his heart. But, every evening, he would be brought back down to Earth by his parent's constant jeering, undermining his self confidence a little more every day. What terrible damage they inflicted upon their own son in these teenage days which should have been so special but were, instead, quite horrible. Every night, he retired to his own room, not wishing to converse with his parents for a minute longer than was absolutely necessary. There he would enter into his alternative world of private daydreams, where everything was as it should be. There was also a spiritual side emerging in John and he started to think more and more about the purpose of life in general. Sometimes he would visit the library and thumb through books on philosophy. He didn't know what he was looking for, but he felt sure that there was a better life somewhere, if only it could be uncovered.

One day, John Brown found his first job, as an assistant in a tailors and drapery store, one of a small chain of such stores in the east end of London. The wages were small, but it got John out of the house and among other people who, he immediately realised, were somewhat different from his parents and he started to glimpse a different life. Arthur's attitude towards his son seemed to change a little for the better now that John had a job. However, more than half of his already meagre wages had to be paid to his mother to help with the housekeeping and Elsie was, by nature, never satisfied. Consequently, the arguments between her and John would continue throughout this period.

John Brown worked hard during his days at the drapery shop and was eventually promoted to a more senior position where he would be entrusted with sales to regular and important clients. He remained shy among others, but was honest and reliable. This was noticed and many expressed a liking towards John. After a year or two, he was promoted again, this time to be head of sales for gentlemen's tailoring. He worked hard and was considered an asset to the company. Indeed, the attitude shown to him at work was quite different from that which he had experienced at home. This made John think increasingly about finding lodgings of his own somewhere and leaving home. After all, his wages would be just enough to allow for this now. However, he found this more difficult than expected and he was only finally able to leave home at the age of twenty.

In the meantime, he met a number of people at his workplace, including some females. However, he remained intensely shy with girls and, even if he persuaded one to come out with him, perhaps to the pictures, or for a walk, it usually ended in disaster, as he simply had no idea how to converse properly with his companions. This was a source of endless anxiety for John Brown, as he was both fascinated by, and much attracted to, young women and would have loved to have had a proper relationship with a female companion. He saw other young men boasting about the relationships that they had with their girlfriends, and was disgusted by their base attitudes towards women and sex. He saw women quite differently, as vulnerable human beings who should be loved, cherished and protected. He was ashamed for his friends when they boasted about their sexual activities, true or otherwise, and nothing else. None of them ever mentioned their love for their girl friends. This seemed alien to John. But then, he had no success at all with girls. They all seemed to shun him, just as people usually shun those who are shy or different in some way, even if this difference is one of basic decency. The truth was that John, perhaps as a result of his lonely childhood, was a deep thinker who read and was, intellectually, years ahead of his peers.

Had he been born into a wealthy, well to do family with loving parents and other siblings, things might have been different. He would have had much more experience with relationships of all kinds and the special relationship between a man and a woman would have been explained to him by his parents. Furthermore, he would have seen such relationships working well in practice and would come to understand and respect the special roles played naturally by males and females. This, in turn, would have set him much more at ease in the company of the opposite sex. Within such a family, he would have been well educated and would certainly have progressed to a suitable university, where he would have come into contact with plenty of females of a similar status to himself, with whom he would, no doubt, have easily mixed. In addition, within the campus environment, he would have had plenty of time to observe his female peers and, consequently, to get to know them properly, without expectations on either side.

Had he been born in ancient Egypt, he would have been taught to respect women and would have understood the different roles played by the sexes, with the man as the provider and the woman as the homemaker. He would have also understood the female contribution to the arts, both in textiles, the graphic arts, music and dance. His teenage days would therefore have been filled with wonder as he discovered all these things and also felt the pangs within his own heart. The ancient Egyptians were family oriented and relationships between family members were extremely important, as were the relationships between prospective husbands and wives.

If John had been born into a culture which did not respect women and considered them as mere objects to facilitate childbirth, then he would have been in an entirely different position. In all probability, his marriage would have been arranged beforehand, to someone who he had never met. His wife may even have been bought and sold as part of a larger transaction. Before this time, any association with women would have been illicit, irresponsible and completely void of any natural affection. In such societies, illegitimate children are rife. As a consequence, affairs of the heart would have meant nothing to him. He would have looked upon his wife as someone who was there to serve him and perform various duties within the household. He may well have entertained various mistresses outside of this relationship. All of this would no doubt have occurred within his late teenage days. Such cultures, who do not respect women, are devoid of love. There is little affection within their close relationships which, in turn, renders them callous and unfeeling as human beings. It is no surprise that such cultures are known for their cruelty and inhumanity. How could they be otherwise, when they have no love or respect for their own wives? It has been written that it is a woman's vocation to inspire love. A beautiful thought. But it can only happen within a cultural environment which allows for it. Even today, in cultures which once understood this, the aggressive drive for material equality and the discrimination against men in many walks of life, are destroying this most beautiful aspect of human relationships. Women are increasingly, no longer allowed to be the feminine underpinnings to family life. This is a tragedy as it eliminates those most precious of qualities of natural life, love and devotion. Many animals understand this. It is only humans who are bleaching out of their cultures of greed.

However, for John Brown, the understanding was there and he yearned for an opportunity to express his love and share his dreams with a like minded young lady. For such an individual, he would have walked through fire and devoted his whole life. But times were changing, even in John Brown's days, and, in his teenage days, it seemed impossible to find the young woman of his dreams. On the few occasions when he did meet someone, he was invariably disappointed.

And so, the teenage days were days of frustration and disappointment with the world in general. The lack of professional success and the inability to forge the sort of deep and lasting relationships, of all kinds, which he so craved, gnawed away at John relentlessly. This would surely affect his own personality, leaving him cynical, suspicious and doing nothing to dispel his shyness. He had in fact, even as a teenager, become introverted, focusing as much upon his own inner world as the world outside. For his inner world was one of aesthetic appreciation and love. Love especially for nature and the natural world. While the outside world seemed like a world of coarseness, greed and shallow relationships. However, as with most teenagers, these thoughts and feelings were mixed together in an inner kaleidoscope, integrated with suspicion, anxiety, anger and a myriad of of other emotions, sometimes waxing and waning from day to day. Such are the complex factors which gel together to form individual personality. It could all have easily been so different for John Brown, had he been born in a different era, in a different land and within, perhaps a different culture. But the laws of probability are inscrutable and we find ourselves where we find ourselves. And we live out our days accordingly. John Brown was just beginning to understand this reality as his teenage days marched inexorably towards their close. So far, it had all happened so swiftly, but what would the future bring?

4. Working Days

John Brown had struggled through his teenage days and, at the age of twenty, had finally made the break with home. His meagre wages just made it possible to rent an extremely modest bed-sitter, in a Victorian terraced house, just off the Commercial Road in London's East End. Now, he was on his own and had to adjust to independence and survival in the big city. His wages hardly allowed him to save anything, once his lodging, travelling and other essential costs were met. He lived a frugal existence and watched where every penny went. The little that he could put by, he placed in a savings account at a local branch of Lloyds Bank. Its accumulation was slow enough. However, John Brown was making it work and was enjoying his independence. He was extremely well organised, in stark contrast with his parents, and lived a tidy, well-ordered life. He started to read much more and established the beginnings of his own small library. And he listened to the radio a great deal, educating himself about the classical music which he was never exposed to as a child. On Sundays, he liked to visit the British Museum and the National Portrait Gallery and never became tired of the exhibits therein. He secretly hoped that he might meet an eligable young lady who might share his view of the world and, with whom, he might enjoy a passionate, romantic relationship. But the opportunity never occurred.

At work, John's dedication and utter reliability stood him in good stead and, eventually, he was entrusted to manage one of the smaller branches of the chain. This meant a slight increase in salary, which was appreciated, but still meant that John was held below the remuneration line which would have enabled him to consider buying a house. As his early working days ticked by, this reality bothered him a great deal. But how could he break out of this relentless routine which, by now, was becoming quite boring and soul-destroying.

On one occasion, John noticed an advertisement, claiming that new people were required for the fledgling electronics industry where, apparently, they could earn high wages and have a definite career path as the industry expanded. To be considered for training, would be entrants had to sit an exam. John inquired further and agreed to attend an examination session one evening at a major London hotel. In the days leading up to this date, he became increasingly excited, daydreaming about his new found career in electronics and how this would change his life completely. On the day, he hurried along after work to the hotel in question, where, after following some signs to the 'Westminster Suite' he found a large gathering of what seemed to be around a hundred or so other young men. Some were assembled in little groups, chatting happily to each other, seemingly without a care in the world. John stood on his own by the wall and watched the scenes around him with interest, but remained separate from them. Eventually, two important looking men entered the room, accompanied by four or five young ladies carrying bundles of paper. One of the men called for quiet and then introduced his colleague, a leading professor of electronics, who explained the procedure for completing the examination paper, with no conferring of any kind, and then handing them in at the desk. With the examination completed, a two hour break would ensue while the papers were quickly scanned, after which, those who had been chosen for further training would be announced.

John sat down with his questionnaire and started answering the questions one by one. Some of them, it seemed, could have had more than one answer, depending upon your conception of what was being discussed. Many of the questions were dealing with matters of logic and seemed simple enough. Some of them were purely mathematical in scope and required solving. John worked his way through and just managed to reach the end in the allotted time. The papers were gathered up and, at this point, quite a few of the attendees left, presumably because they felt that they had not done well on the paper. John was mildly confident however, just as he had been in his eleven plus examination, and decided to stay behind and wait for the results.

The two hours passed very slowly indeed until, at last, the two men entered the room again, one of them holding a handful of papers. They thanked everyone for attending and offered their commiserations to those who would not, on this occasion, be selected. John waited with baited breath as the names of the lucky ones were read out and the individuals concerned assembled close to the makeshift stage area, where one of the girls ticked off their names. John listened very attentively, waiting for the name 'John Brown' which would surely be annunciated soon. The reader paused for a moment or two, looked at the paper, and then thanked everyone again for attending, before leaving the stage. John had not been selected and his heart sank. He had a feeling of failure and inadequacy, such as he had never felt before and, together with a few tens of others, shuffled out of the building and on to the adjacent street outside. Some of those who had failed had, once again, assembled in little groups and were discussing why they thought they had failed the questionnaire. John Brown, as usual, remained alone and slowly made his way to the nearest London Underground station in order to return home to his small bed sitting room. Once at home, he made a cup of tea and sat down to reflect on the experience. No matter how he tried, he could not shake off the heavy weight of failure which pressed down upon him. Why could he have not been one of the chosen ones? What was it about him which made him fail where others so easily succeeded? This experience hurt him deeply and, the next day, he returned to the drudgery of managing the shop.

And so, John Brown's working life continued, with few memorable events. Often, he felt that his life was slipping through his fingers as time rolled on and he seemed to achieve nothing at all. He enjoyed no success in his romantic life, as the girls he met all seemed to be shy and did not communicate effectively with him, or perhaps it was the other way around. Either way, he simply did not connect in any meaningful way with women. He loved and cherished them dearly and felt very protective towards them, but they seemed wary and distant, as though this was not what they wanted. But then, what did they want? John could never quite understand this conundrum. One trend which did emerge during these days, was that others who were misfits in society, for whatever reason, seemed to find their way to John. Perhaps it was because of his eternal patience and kindness towards those less fortunate than himself. Perhaps it was because he knew himself what it was to be lonely. In any event, several such individuals, who everybody else would shun, would attach themselves to John and, to his credit, he never turned them away. He sensed a deeper understanding in some of these individuals, despite their idiosyncrasies, and they, in turn, were grateful to John for his patience and friendship.

Life continued and John Brown wondered whether he would spend the rest of his working days managing drapery and clothing stores in London's east end. But then, one cold November day when winter was just beginning to bite, fate stepped in when the director of the firm visited John's branch and informed him that, as of the next day, the company was closing its doors and going into liquidation. John Brown and all of his working colleagues would be redundant from the close of business on that day. This news fell like a hammer upon John. There was just one weeks extra closing pay and that was that. John would have to seek another job and, in the meantime, sign on the list of unemployed.

In those days, there was a huge stigma attached to being unemployed, and this was felt keenly by those who, like John, wanted to work and get on in life, but who had been poorly educated and had no professional qualifications at all. There was nothing for it, John Brown had become one of the nation's unemployed and had to visit the unemployment office every week in order to sign the register and receive a pittance of a benefit which, in John's case, hardly paid the rent and left very little with which to eat and seek work. John felt deeply ashamed of his situation and tried, desperately, to seek work of any kind that would pay his rent and keep him going. But the more he tried, the harder it became to find work, as weeks slipped by and became months. Every advertisement that he responded to yielded nothing and the unemployment office could offer no suitable vacancies. The pressure and dismay that such a situation inflicted upon its sufferers was immense and John felt it more than most. The blow to his self-confidence was significant and such that he would never quite recover from it. His sense of loneliness became accentuated and it was as if he stood alone within an unsympathetic world in which, it was becoming increasingly clear, he had no place.

And then, one day, the unemployment office alerted John to an opportunity with the Shoreditch Construction Company, who needed and office administrator and storeman. John knew nothing at all about the building and construction business, but he pursued every opportunity relentlessly and, on a

Thursday late afternoon he attended an interview with a Mr Timms, who was co-owner of the relatively small business, his partner being a Mr Barker, who could not be present at the time. Timms and Barker were both hands-on types who enjoyed being on site and hated being in the office. They desperately needed someone reliable who could manage things in an orderly manner at their base office. John explained his past employment history to Mr Timms and, when asked what he knew about the construction business, replied truthfully that he knew nothing. "But you could learn" suggested Timms and John answered in the affirmative. Timms liked John right from the start and detected his inherent honesty and dependability. Not being one to waste time, he rose from his chair, instructed John to come back and start work first thing on the following Monday, and then held the door open for John, before following him out on to the street. "I think you will fit in" he exclaimed as he headed off down the street and a bewildered, but happy John headed home. At last, after eighteen months of unemployment, the tide had turned and John, once again, had a job. He determined that he would spend the weekend learning all he could about the construction business, although there was little available to help him at this time. The library had no books on the subject and the best he could do was to visit some operational sites and simply observe, as best he could, what was going on. He was slightly concerned about his lack of inside knowledge and, in fact, did not really understand what his knew job actually was. Mr Timms had mentioned the management of plans and keeping an eye on the store, but, beyond this, John had no idea of his forthcoming duties. There was, at the office, a secretary, a mature lady by the name of Mrs Reading. No doubt she could steer John in his early days.

John Brown duly turned up for the first day at his new job and found a general disarray with regard to filing and accessibility of information. Mrs Reading tended to manage the reception area and keep an eye on the accounts, but she could not manage everything and welcomed John's presence on the scene. He spent his first few days becoming familiar with the firm's business practices, what sort of jobs they accepted and how they operated. It quickly became clear that stores management was an issue and, often, time would be wasted on site due to the non-availability of basic materials. By the end of his first week, John had drawn up an inventory of the stores and developed a simple system for keeping the fundamental materials always in stock. He presented his ideas to Timms and Barker when they called him in to ask how he was progressing. John explained the principles of his system and suggested that holding larger stocks of everyday materials might actually save them money, from both a procurement and operational perspective. Oddly, his years in the drapery and clothing business had prepared him quite well to deal with such matters. He further explained that he was in the process of creating a sensible filing system for plans, based upon place name, rather than date, enabling pertinent information to be quickly found. Mr Timms and Mr Barker looked at each other in astonishment. This was exactly what they needed. What a stroke of luck to come across this John Brown character.

John dovetailed easily into his new role and, in contrast to his days in the drapery, was actually enjoying it most of the time. Timms and Barker were pleased with him and it was not long before his salary was raised and, for the first time in his life, John felt that he needn't be constantly worried about his finances. However, he remained at the low end of the scale of paid employees and still had to be careful. Nevertheless, he entered into his new duties and new life with somewhat more enthusiasm than he had previously been able to muster. But the future remained unclear.

Had John Brown been born into a well to do, upper class family, his future would have been very clear. It would have been decided upon while he was still at secondary school, if not before, and, having done exceptionally well in the sixth form at school, he would have entered the university of his choice in order to obtain the appropriate qualifications. Even while at university, he would have been approached by organisations or government agencies, keen to acquire his skills as soon as he was qualified. He would have walked out of the university, straight into a well paid, prestigious position, in which he would quickly flourish and make his mark. Financial insecurity would be a concept with which he would have been unfamiliar. He would probably inherit property of his own and would no doubt have a choice of living accommodation, perhaps in the town as well as the country. Fairly quickly, he would have married, a girl with suitable prospects and from the right family. Love would not be a primary factor although, naturally, he would have some empathy with his wife, whose main role would be to produce children and administer the domestic side of things.

If he had been born into the upper classes of any of the ancient civilisations, his future would have been similarly assured from a young age. He would have dutifully followed the customs of his country, perpetuating the culture through to the next generation. He would, no doubt, have lived in luxury with all of his requirements attended to by a suitable number of staff. He would have little empathy with classes outside of his own, for his own situation provided him with everything that he could possibly need. He would have an arranged marriage to at least one wife and would probably see nothing wrong with maintaining at least a few mistresses if that was what amused him. He would almost certainly not be burdened with concepts such as true love, as such would simply be an annoyance and a hindrance to the flow of the inevitable.

He might have been born into a a Lapland or Bakhtiari family, in which case, his future would be inextricably bound to that of the animals upon which they depended. He would roam with the family across many lands and, as he did so, learn the necessary skills with which to survive, in sometimes quite hostile environments. He would have little or no academic exposure but would learn, by word of mouth, the history of his people, punctuated with stories of great events. He would marry a suitable bride and she would look after the family as well as participate in the everyday activities of the group. There would be no permanent home, only the barest of essentials with regards clothing and tools.

Or maybe he would be born into a poor family in a small village in India, where he would live a very basic agricultural lifestyle with very little expectation of ever having a conventional job. He would have enjoyed an arranged marriage with as much ceremony as his little village could muster, and he would have been generally happy enough, with strong religious beliefs to shape his inner thoughts and outward behaviour, Such strong beliefs, together with the caste system, would occasionally lead him into situations of conflict. The struggle for existence would have lead him to adopt ways which we would call dishonest, grasping and calculating and yet, to him, would simply be everyday life. His wife and children would have worked, sometimes much harder than he himself, in everyday matters of survival.

Perhaps he might have been born a prince or the son of a duke in eighteenth century Europe. His work, such as it would have been, would consist mainly of keeping up appearances at state or private balls. Being seen in all the great houses and in the upper stratas of society. He might have occasionally dabbled in politics and would certainly have wanted a say in local affairs. His wealth would have been such that he would rarely even think about the sordid subject of money, except when it would have been owed to him of course. He would have been married with great aplomb to a society lady of equal standing, no doubt, with a prodigious amount of money changing hands as a dowry.

But no, John Brown was born in the London Hospital to working class parents and grew up in the east end of London. His life may have continued, albeit in a modest manner, in the employment of Timms and Barker, had fate not taken a hand one damp Friday in February when he was called into the office of Mr Timms and it was explained to him that his services would no longer be required. For Timms and Barker had made the mistake, as many businesses do, of perpetually paying their bills either at the last minute or late. As their suppliers started to react by limiting their credit, they found that they could simply not catch up and settle their accounts and so, reluctantly, the Shoreditch Construction Company was dissolved and John Brown, once again, found himself redundant.

He was familiar with the unemployment routine. The shame of having to queue up with other men in order to sign the register and receive a pittance on which he could hardly survive. It was as though he was being punished for becoming unemployed. He reasoned that, if he worked for himself, this would not happen, but he had no trade and no capital with which to start a business. Furthermore, he could not afford to take the time to learn a trade which, in any event, would be hard now at his age. He was forced therefore to seek employment and entered into the familiar, degrading routine of scouring the newspapers and calling in at employment agencies in order to seek a position. Once again, his self confidence was shattered and he felt the pain of being alone in the world and, to all intents and purposes, unwanted. He countered this, to some extent, by reading and reasoning that the same thing had happened to many other people and that there was really no disgrace attached to his situation.

Nevertheless, he was becoming unnerved by the situation as the weeks rolled by and became months. He took to walking the streets in order that he would at least be among others, although this only served to heighten his predicament.

His salvation finally came, after fourteen months, when he gained employment as a clerk in the firm of Septimus Fogg and Company, shipping agents, in Burr Street by Saint Katherine Dock. Fogg and Company was a well established firm with good credentials and John was relieved that he was finally working for a substantial company. His skills in record keeping and organisation would find a ready outlet at Fogg's and he quickly became a valued member of staff. It was hard work and John often stayed late in order to complete his tasks, but it was a satisfying position none the less. He realised that there was little scope for advancement. A shipping clerk was a shipping clerk and that was that. But he at least had a job and could support himself once more.

Time slipped by quickly at Fogg and Company, with months melting into years while John Brown remained a humble shipping clerk, albeit an experienced and competent one. In time, he managed to secure himself a Council flat in the area and generally improved his living conditions. From time to to time, he would make a concerted effort to mix socially and, especially, seek the company of ladies. However, he remained unsuccessful in his quest. No doubt partly because he was not really the socialising type. His childhood and subsequent experiences had caused him to become self sufficient in every way and, in truth, he often preferred to be by himself than in the company of others. He was quite happy to simply listen to the radio or read one of his books, rather than to engage in the complications of socialising with others. He was lonely and often yearned for company but, when he did find it, he never quite knew what to say and felt awkward. Consequently, time after time, he would retreat into the relative safety of his own private, lonely world.

The years slowly ticked by and John Brown became something of a fixture at Septimus Fogg and Company, where he was known by all their clients as a reliable and helpful individual. They had no idea of his private life and the long cold nights spent alone in his flat. Such were the working days of John Brown. In fact, there were hundreds, just like John, scattered across London, in flats and guest houses. It was an unforgiving city for those whose shyness lead to solitude.

5. Private Days

While John Brown's working life had stabilised and he felt reasonably secure in his job as a shipping clerk, his private life was a different matter altogether. Inwardly, John was an affectionate man with strong principles of integrity. He desperately wanted to find love and to honour and care for a lady with similar principles as himself. However, in John Brown's time, it was not so easy to meet such individuals if you were not well connected yourself. He tried going to clubs and dance halls, but he was shy and, in any case, the young ladies that he did take a liking to were always with someone else. He tried visiting art galleries and museums, but found it extremely difficult to open a conversation with anyone and, on the rare occasions when he did so, the other party promptly closed it again and walked out of his life. This abject failure in befriending members of the opposite sex was something which caused John a great deal of anguish. No matter how much he tried, he could never win the friendship of any suitable young lady. As the years rolled by and he became older, he acknowledged that he was simply not destined for a loving relationship, no matter how much he dreamed and yearned for one. In fact, he knew very few people at all outside of his few colleagues at Fogg and Company. He had a nodding acquaintance with one or two of his neighbours at the small block of Council flats where he lived, but they never asked him in. Similarly, he knew one or two people in the shops that he visited regularly but, while he got along very well with them, he could not consider them friends in the true sense of the word.

One of the problems was that John had interests outside of his class. While others liked football and going to public houses, John preferred to visit museums and galleries. While others enjoyed the popular music of the day, John preferred to listen to classical music and was, in fact, becoming quite knowledgeable on the subject. But of course, he was branded as working class and would not be likely to meet with those who shared his more civilised interests. He continued to buy and read interesting books, including the classics, and had bought an inexpensive record player in order to play his favourite pieces. Consequently, John was never bored, but he did retreat, more and more, into his private world. He daydreamed about the man he would have liked to have been, but remained the man he was, locked in a time and place and defined by his background and accent. These attributes confined him as surely as prison walls. He was indeed a prisoner of circumstance.

His human relationships might have been so different. Had he been born into an established, well to do family, he would undoubtedly have had a brace of siblings, cousins and other relatives, with whom he would have been constantly engaging, building up his social skills accordingly. By the time he attended school, he would already possess the necessary self confidence to make friends and forge lasting relationships. Furthermore, he would have been exposed, from an early age, to the company of girls and would not have been shy in their presence. On the contrary, he would have found their friendship intriguing and would have enjoyed being with them. By the time he left the sixth form and was heading for university, he would already have started to have serious relationships with young ladies, providing the opportunity to develop his natural affections in that direction. By the time he left university, he probably would have forged a very special relationship with a young lady, and would be thinking about marriage. The eventual marriage ceremony would be a joyful occasion, shared with family and friends and, after an equally joyous honeymoon, he would have settled down into a blissful, loving relationship with his wife. He would maintain his other friendships and, together with his wife, would enjoy a full and enduring social life.

Had he been born into a different culture, perhaps in the east, he would have had an arranged marriage, with the bride being selected, probably while he was still a boy. The relationship would have been somewhat different as he would have had a different perspective with regard to women. He would expect his wife to run the household and attend to all domestic matters, while he engaged in whatever business or professional activity he had entered into. The choice of bride would have been made according to class and social standing, and so, at least his wife and himself would be of a similar background and would come to an appropriate understanding. He may even begin to regard her with affection and care for her as time passed by.

He might have been born into a traditional European culture a hundred years or so before, wherein women were regarded as the fairer sex and were revered accordingly. He would have been educated in his manner towards women, always placing them before himself and, as a matter of honour, doing his very best to protect and care for them. Having fallen in love with an eligible young lady, he would have entered into a very formal courtship, probably under the discretion of the mother or a doting aunt, and would have exercised perfect manners towards his intended bride and her relations. However, these manners were not just a matter of custom. They would be ingrained into his principles and he would genuinely look upon his loved one as the most precious aspect of his own life. He would walk through fire for her if necessary and would love her with all his heart, until death do them part. This would be the way of a gentleman and, if John Brown had been born into such a family, then a gentleman he would be. He would protect, love and cherish his wife and she, in turn, would love him and attend to his domestic life in every detail. This, indeed, would be what was expected in any marriage.

Perhaps he might have been born into a culture, past or present, that shows no respect at all for women, denying them basic rights and treating them simply as property of the man. If brought up in such a culture, he may well have perpetuated such an injustice, especially if it were to his benefit. He might have traded women as he would horses. He would expect them to attend to his every need, but would never value them as individuals and the concept of love for a woman would be alien to him.

But John was none of these and was simply a lonely working class man who loved women, but did not posses the social skills necessary to mix successfully with them or to attract them. It was the same with friendships in general. He had had no brothers or sisters and had grown up in a loveless household where he was made to feel of no importance. His experiences at the schools which he attended, simply served to reinforce this feeling and, while he was capable of performing his working roles and responsibilities, he could somehow never carry this forward into his private life. This was a tragedy, as John was, like many such individuals, at heart a very affectionate and honourable person. He would have made a good husband and been a loyal friend to anyone who became close.

One summer Sunday, as John was sitting in his flat with the balcony door open, a ginger cat walked in and eyed him up and down. A surprised John spoke to the cat and then provided him with a saucer of milk, which was gratefully accepted. The cat stayed with John for an hour or so, and then disappeared. Every now and again, but especially at weekends, the cat would appear, and became increasingly friendly. Indeed, John started to buy him little tins of sardines and assorted cat food and would always have something for him when he visited. He had no idea where the cat came from or who his owner was, but John named him Peter and enjoyed his company. In truth, John looked forward to Peter's visits enormously and would spend many hours talking to him and generally looking after him. It occurred to him, how easy it was to establish a relationship with an animal. Animals were simple and sincere in their relationships and loyal in their friendships. Humans were neither. It seemed to John that human relationships were always complicated and uncertain, and he never managed to forge deep friendships with anyone. With Peter however, he immediately fell into a close and fond relationship which brought him much comfort in his private life. Indeed, he had not realised just how much he had come to depend upon this unusual friendship until, one week, he noticed that Peter had not visited at all. Nor the next week. John went around the nearby streets, searching for some sign of him, but there was nothing. Peter had simply disappeared. Perhaps his owners had moved house. Perhaps something had happened to him. Whatever it was, John was heartbroken. He sadly disposed of the, as yet unused, tins of food, as he could not bear to look at them. Similarly, with Peter's special dish and the cushions on which he used to sit. John's private life now descended into a new level of cold emptiness. He came home in the evenings and listened to his records or read, but there was no enjoyment in these activities any more. He had been exposed to the pure friendship that can only come from an animal and now understood, even more keenly, what his life was missing. He wondered whether he might acquire a pet of his own, but then realised that he was in no position to provide a proper home. He also understood the grief that would undoubtedly come with the loss of such a pet.

And so, sadly, John Brown continued with his uneventful private life. Always dreaming. Always hoping. But never fulfilling his ambitions for friendship.

John liked to listen to music from Corelli, Telemann, Boccherini, Reicha and others and he liked to look, in his books, at paintings by Botticelli, Giotto and the impressionists Renoir and Van Gogh. He loved beautiful things and liked to immerse himself in beautiful thoughts. Thoughts about nature. Thoughts about humanity. Thoughts about the love of life. Sometimes, when in such a frame of mind, he would feel the tears run down his cheeks and drip on to his shirt, and then, was immediately ashamed at showing such emotion. In any event, they were tears of which no one was aware, and for which no one cared. They came from a place deep down in John's soul. A cold, dark, desolate place, which had never been illuminated by the warmth of love. They would be understood only by those who had, themselves, plumbed the depths of loneliness and despair.

Sometimes, John would tell himself that his social predicament was entirely his own fault and that he should get out and engage with other people. Only then would he stand a chance of meeting potential friends, including perhaps, those of the opposite gender. And so, he would smarten himself up as best he could and force himself to go out in the evenings and at weekends, visiting public houses, going to the cinema and even attending ballrooms where couples would dance the night away. He would go and stand among groups who were deep in discussion and would, occasionally, volunteer a comment or suggestion, only to be met with a cool glance. Once or twice at the ballrooms, with enormous difficulty, he would summon the courage to ask a young lady if she would like to dance, but was always politely refused. He was, after all, getting a little old for such things and his appearance seemed to unsettle those who were younger and living in a different world. But then, no one seemed to live in John's world. And so, he would always end up walking home alone and returning to his flat. Retreating to his own world, where he was at home with his music, literature and his own thoughts. Such were the private days of John Brown.

6. Later Days

Time may be relative, but it rolls inexorably forwards and waits for no man. There were days when John Brown worried keenly about the passing of time and his continued lack of success in all things. He felt that he had achieved nothing at all and had simply been existing. Others accomplished great things and were admired by their peers and by ordinary people. Some were successful socially and had many friends and acquaintances, as well as being happily married. Others were successful in business, amassing small fortunes along the way. But John Brown was absent from all of these groups. Even when he tried some volunteering work, they soon found that they didn't need him. It seemed that he was forever destined to remain John Brown, shipping agent and nobody in particular. But now the years were stacking up and John was gazing down the road at the latter half of his life on Earth. He would continue to work at his job, although the big docks were closing down now and there was little actual shipping taking place on the Thames. However, it seemed that many in the area continued to require the services of a shipping agent, even if the actual shipping was taking place at Southampton, Harwich, Liverpool and elsewhere. In addition, there was a growing amount of air freight coming and going from London Airport, Southend Airport and others. In short, there was plenty of work for a London based shipping agent and so, Fogg and Company continued to prosper from their crowded office in Burr Street.

It was when John was not working that the reality of his situation spoke to him the loudest. He would look back on his life and realise that he had few happy memories to take into account. It was a life punctuated by frustration and loneliness. A life of good intentions that never materialised. A soul of affection and sensitivity that never saw the light of day. He had no friends in the real sense. just his acquaintances at the office and a cautious nodding relationship with his neighbours. And so, he would cast his thoughts to his daydreams of what might have been and lose himself in his hobbies of music and literature. Sometimes, in the evenings after work and often on Sundays he would walk along the banks of the Thames. Along St Katherine Street and into Tower Wharf, where he would always spend a minute or so looking up at the Tower of London and wonder how many eyes had seen the same sight, through good times and bad, in winter and in summer. Some might have caught a last glimpse of the Tower as they boarded a small boat and rowed back down the Thames to escape some persecution or other. Some may have looked up in admiration as they drifted slowly up river in rowed barges, bound for one of the large estates whose land bordered the great river. John imagined all sorts of adventures as he strolled by this emblem of London. Further on he would walk, coming to the embankment proper, where he might half cross one of the bridges in order to gaze down upon the swirling waters. It was a beautiful sight, especially in the early evening mist of the autumn months.

John Brown had not really had any proper holidays. When his annual leave came around, he would usually remain in London, his home town, for which he held a certain, robust affection, without really understanding why. He would spend his time visiting the big museums in Kensington, discovering new art galleries; he loved to visit the small galleries who were often gracious enough to speak to him about their exhibits. He would look in all the shops in Bond Street and Regent Street and he loved to visit Regents Park, where he would sit down on the grass and watch the world pass by. Sometimes, he would take a picnic lunch with him, usually a couple of bread rolls with cheese and pickle, and a small bottle of cider. He would then tune in his pocket radio to the third programme and enjoy a pleasant hour or so. On one occasion, he decided to have a more formal holiday and booked a place at a guest house in the Lake District. He enjoyed the train journey, from Euston, winding its way up through the midlands and, eventually, to Penrith station. There he hired a taxi for the long ride to his guest house in Ambleside, in the very heart of the Lake District. Once there, he quickly realised that he had come unprepared and had to shop locally for hiking boots and a decent storm coat.

John Brown enjoyed chatting with the other residents at the guest house, although they had very little in common. Most of the others were experienced walkers and had a very good knowledge of the area. John absorbed what he could from them and, once equipped with the basic necessities, bought a packed lunch from the guest house and set out on his first walk around the lakes and up on the fells. He enjoyed his four days of walking and became accustomed to the typical Lake District weather of sunny spells and unpredictable showers as the clouds rolled in from the west. The scenery was very different from London and John soaked it all up enthusiastically. The problem was, of course, that he had no companion with whom to share his adventures or his aesthetic appreciation of the countryside. He would often talk to himself, in his mind, as he climbed the fells and looked out across the beautiful landscape. Sometimes he would invent an imaginary companion, to whom he would point out what he saw and explain the significance of it. In truth, although he loved the countryside, he was still chained by his loneliness and so could not be truly happy. When he finally disembarked the train at Euston and made his way back, on the underground, to his council flat in the East End, he was relieved and grateful to be home. When he totted up the cost of this one week excursion, including the train and taxi fares, the cost of his lodgings, his food and clothing expenses, and so on, he realised that it had also made a sizable indentation in his savings. From then on, his leave periods were all spent in London. After all, there was always something new to discover in this colourful, historic city.

And so, John Brown's later days closely resembled his earlier days in every detail. It might have been very different, had he been born into a well to do upper class family, in which case, his academic training would have prepared him for a professional life with a clearly defined path of advancement. By now, he would be very well established in his chosen career, perhaps as a biologist, a geologist or other scientist, perhaps as a medical doctor, perhaps as an ambassador, perhaps in one of the armed services. In any event, he would have undertaken many important tasks and given his name to many important papers. He may, depending upon profession, may have spoken at important international conferences and liaised internationally with other groups. Certainly, his name would, by now, be well recognised within his chosen field of endeavour.

Had he been born into one of the ancient civilisations, a similar path of achievement would have been followed and his name would have been widely known and respected. Indeed, by now, he would be involved in important matters concerning community or state and would be proud of his responsibilities and his execution of them. If he had been born much later, but to a good family in Europe, he would undoubtedly have been involved in some sort of professional activity and would have been proud to carry his family name forward, as indeed would have been expected of him. If he had been born at a time which meant going to war, he would have served his country with distinction as an officer and a gentleman.

Alternatively, he might have been born into a poor agricultural family, perhaps in the Middle East or even further east. He might have been a simple shepherd. However, he would have learned how to be a good shepherd and would be taking pride in his life's work. By now, he would be respected within the community as a knowledgeable elder, from whom others could, and would, learn. The same would be true within many simple communities who lived off the land, wherever they might be situated. There would be respect shown for years of dedication to the community and for the preservation of its culture. At either end of the material scale, this natural order of things would be maintained. But John Brown fell into neither grouping. He was stuck in a no-man's land in the middle, where there was no career path, no community involvement and no recognition. Furthermore, other than unexpected luck, there was no career path for him to follow and no opportunity to contribute, in any meaningful sense, to the industry of which he was a very small part. He was one of life's countless nobodies which made up a fair proportion of western society. The faceless individuals which served, unnoticed, behind shop counters, in offices or as lowly tradespeople. They were, in fact, an important component within the overall economy, but they were of no importance themselves. When they retired, there was a steady supply of others to fill the gap.

The later days of John Brown were thus just further steps along an inevitable path of darkness and anonymity. There would be no special highlights, no recognition, nothing in particular to lift the spirits. And there would be no glowing warmth of affection or deep friendship. Just a long, lonely, winding path into an unknown future. Looking back, down along a very similar path, John could harbour many regrets and yet, he had had so few options that most of his regrets were not of his own making. They were more concerned with accidents of birth. Those from similar backgrounds who had been extraordinarily lucky in life would claim, unintelligently, that anyone can achieve whatever they want and that people make their own luck. People like John Brown would understand however, that this simply is not the case. And the days run inexorably from one to the next.

7. Last Days

The path of life winds on and, for better or for worse and barring accidents, one finds oneself in that last quarter of life when, suddenly, all that has gone before seems like just a flash of existence and one realises that the end is beckoning. Depending on the experiences encountered along the way, this may encourage feelings of warm reflections or a sensation more akin to panic, as the realisation of one's past life seeps in and there seems to be very little on the positive side of the balance sheet. But how can this be if everything balances out under nature?

In ancient Egypt, there was a belief that, after death, the soul would, after its initial journey, find itself at the gates of the temple of Osiris and Isis where it would be subject to the weighing of the heart ceremony. This ceremony would be officiated by the faithful servant and dweller of the tomb, Anubis, the jackal headed God. Like those of his kind and just like wolves and dogs today, Anubis could not be fooled and understood your true heart. And so, the deceased's heart would be weighed on the scales against the feather, representing all of the good deeds undertaken by the deceased. If the scales balanced, the soul would be admitted into the temple of Osiris and Isis. If they did not, the soul would be committed to the underworld, where it must roam for eternity. This is a lovely idea which reinforces the belief that there is more to life than power, position and material gain.

But what are these other qualities or experiences which will help the scales to balance? For many, they will be aligned with the soul, or inner self. That entity which provides us with a conscience and a belief in the necessity of moral values. We can live without these things, as many millions of people do, but they reflect the true values of life. Perhaps the ancient Egyptians, and many others since, would argue that the purpose of life is to acquire knowledge and understanding and to utilise these qualities in the service of others. Let them be manifested in kindness and compassion towards all those in need. Some people align these qualities with religion, but they are, in fact, quite separate and may be readily practised by anyone, religious or otherwise. In many cultures, monks and nuns, or their equivalents, have made this association with religion and, mostly, used it to good purpose. There are many examples where they have helped the poor and destitute and equally many examples where they have not. One does not need to claim a religious allegiance in order to be a fundamentally good person. Many people are naturally good and spend their lives helping others, both humans and animals. Others are naturally greedy and callous and do nothing that is not for their immediate profit. Ironically, it is often the latter who are recognised by society and who believe that they are successful human beings. They even deride others who do not follow this path and, unfortunately, the modern world seems to have set its course firmly along this trajectory. Consequently, those who are honest and would never do anything to hurt another individual, often are those who do not get on in the world, depending of course upon their background and education. One would like to suppose that all those who are properly educated would understand this and would follow the highest moral rigour. But this is simply not the case, as we see with so many of our politicians and successful business men and women.

The John Browns of this world offend no one and achieve nothing. At least, they achieve nothing according to the metrics of the modern world. But maybe they achieve more than they know, in that they perpetuate a natural kindness, tolerance and goodwill, so essential to civilisation. In recent history, we have seen, with the two world wars, what happens when we forget these characteristics. We have born witness to the depths to which humanity can descend. In the last war, it was the John Browns who, in their hundreds of thousands, put on uniforms and stood against the Nazi evil and aggression. So many of them gave their lives anonymously and without any recognition in support of this cause. Throughout his life, if John Brown were to see someone fall over, he would be the first to help them up and check that they were OK. He would seek neither thanks or recognition, but simply continue on his way afterwards. This was a natural reaction to him. His kindness to Peter, the cat, was another expression of this natural empathy with life which is essential to the continuance of civilisation. Those who do not feel this, cannot live a worthwhile life, no matter how many riches or how much power they accumulate.

When John Brown looked back on his life, he was saddened to think that he had achieved nothing. He had left no lasting legacy and had not even had children of his own. It is true that he had contributed very little in a material sense, but perhaps it was not true that he had achieved nothing. Perhaps he was simply part of the larger scale evolutionary churn which perpetuated humanity. Perhaps his soul, and everything that he had learned, would go back into some vast pool of the human life force, thus refining it further. John would often ponder such things as he lived out his last working years at Fogg and Company. By now, he had become the voice of experience at the little offices on Burr Street, as he knew the operation supremely well. But even that knowledge, in the broader scheme of things, meant very little and, surely, no one would remember John Brown, shipping agent clerk. He would look back on his childhood, trying to remember summer days filled with love, but there weren't any. He would think of his school days and the inability of any of the teachers to really explain anything to him. He did remember however the two times that he had become unemployed and the stress that this placed upon him.

The fact that governments are willing to allow many millions of children to grow up like John Brown, while a smaller number benefit from the education and opportunities that should surely be available to everyone, has much to do with their vision of economies and the need to maintain a sizable, uneducated working class. This would seem such a waste of resource as, had John Brown been properly educated, he could have become a much greater asset to society, as a professional man in one area or another. But economists would argue that you cannot have more than a small portion of the population educated, as there would not be the positions for them in society. The counter argument is that, whether there are positions for them or not, it is their right to receive a proper education, including moral guidance. Had this been the case over the past few centuries, across the world, then we would probably not have the population explosion problem which has now become the greatest threat to civilisation. The globalisation of greed has ensured the dilution of cultures to a point which does not promote a sense of belonging in anyone. This might also have been averted with a more widely educated populace. The John Browns of the world are an interesting barometer of civilisation. There are levels below and levels above this point, into which large numbers of the global population fall. If the John Brown position shifts significantly in either direction, then that is surely an indicator of societal wellbeing.

But let us return to John Brown's own story. He was at the stage of his life now where the prospect of retirement was looming large. He had witnessed the situation where his more senior colleagues reached retirement. How much they looked forward to it, counting the days in the last month or so, and how they would discuss all the things that they would do when they retired. Some were looking forward to travelling to all the places that they had heard about but never seen. Some were looking forward to starting ambitious projects in their gardens. Some were simply looking forward to spending more time with their growing families, bouncing grandchildren on their knees and doing all the things that are expected of grandparents. John would enjoy listening to all their plans but, when the retirement date was looming for himself, it created a rather different feeling. He was, in fact, dreading his retirement. After all, the only proper contact he had with other people was through his work. If that was to be taken away, he would have virtually no contact with others. He would still be able to amuse himself with his hobbies and with his visits to the museums and galleries, but it would be a lonely existence without his daily life at Burr Street.

After much apprehension and anticipation, the day finally arrived for John Brown's retirement. The office manager, called everyone together at lunchtime and announced that they were losing a loyal and dependable employee, who they would be sad to see go, although they wished him every happiness in his retirement. He was presented with a nice fold-up travel alarm clock which he thanked the manager for profusely. On realising that he was expected to say a few words himself, he was initially tongue tied with shyness and embarrassment, but overcame the feeling to thank everyone and say how much he had enjoyed his time with the company, and how sad he was to be leaving. And John really meant every word. Others might have left after their presentation, but John Brown stayed at his desk and worked hard to make sure that everything was absolutely in order, before he finally left for home, a little after six o'clock. The last walk away from the office and along Burr Street, filled John's eyes with tears and, by the time he reached home, his face was wet with their tracks. He opened the door and entered his council flat once more, just like he had done a thousand times before, but this time it was different. He felt that he was entering his own tomb.

However, the next day dawned sunny and bright and John Brown began to think that. maybe, retirement wouldn't be so bad after all. He could spend more time at the museums, his favourite being the British Museum where, occasionally, he would chat with one or other of the curators. He had been visiting the British Museum for more than thirty years and many of the curators recognised him and would say a few words. He would also visit the major museums in Kensington and, of course, all the art galleries with which he was familiar. And the libraries and parks. He would find things to keep him busy and retirement would not be so bad.

The reality became rather different as John's days ticked past and merged with one another in a continuous stream of bleakness. The visits to the museums were not the same now. The joy had gone out of it. They were now just notches within a mechanical diary that saw him repeat his footsteps along well-trod paths, again and again. On some days, he did not venture out at all, but sat listening to his records or reading. In the winter months, he had the excuse of the weather to keep him indoors. He was, in fact, becoming increasingly isolated, as many retired people do when they are on their own.

John Brown's life continued along this dreary path for a year or two until, one day, he noticed that he was not so sure of his balance and felt very tired. He shook this off as best he could and even managed a trip to the corner shop to buy in some essential provisions but, on returning home, he sank into his armchair and drifted into a deep sleep. When he awoke, it was late at night and he struggled to put his shopping away and make himself a cup of tea, before going to bed. He rose, later than usual the next day, but did not feel very well. He got as far as lunchtime, when he made himself a sandwich and a cup of tea, but then went back to bed.

The next day, John Brown awoke at around eleven o'clock. He did not know what time it was, but assumed it was early morning and so closed his eyes and went back to sleep. He awoke briefly in the afternoon but by now, did not have any sense of time and slowly drifted back to sleep. The next day, he awoke, with the sun streaming through his window and determined that he would get up and go for a walk. After all, he needed some fresh milk now. But he wouldn't go just yet. Just another half hour, and he would get up. The hours passed and the sun had moved around to the other side of the building now, leaving John's room looking rather bland. He reasoned that he would put his trip off until the next day and fell back to sleep. The next day, the same thing happened, John determined that he would definitely get up today, just a few more minutes in bed. But the day came and went and John remained in his room. On the next day, early in the morning, John awoke and looked around him. Everything seemed a little strange and disjointed. He was aware that he was supposed to do something, but could not remember what. He lay and he drifted. In the afternoon, he felt cold and it seemed dark in his room, but he did not know why. In fact, he did not even know where he was anymore. His legs and hips felt painful, and he was tired. So very tired.

At around seven o'clock in the evening. John Brown passed away and his soul departed this Earth forever. There was no one at his bedside. He had no family or friends. No one even knew that he had died. It was around eight days later when the council had tried to contact him about some repair work to the flat and could not do so, that someone realised something was wrong. The social services team entered the flat and found John's body, on its side and half covered with his blanket. As there were no relatives, the council arranged for John's remains to be cremated and the bank, at a cost, brought his financial arrangements to and end. And that was the end of a life which had meant very little to anyone. John Brown's passing would not be noted anywhere and no one would feel a loss. Very quickly, his name would be forgotten and a new tenant would be installed in the flat after it had been cleared of all John's belongings and redecorated. John Brown's days had come to and end. They had passed away on the outgoing tide, never to return.

John Brown was an ordinary man, His was a hard life, not in the sense that he wanted for nourishment or shelter, but that he was weighed down by the chains of mediocrity and anonymity and, struggle though he might, he could never throw off these chains that rattled with him throughout the course of his life. In later years, they would be joined by a growing millstone of dissatisfaction as he felt that his life had been a failure. But these burdens were not of John Brown's making. They were the facets of a society who did not value those who did not fit into a common model and who did not think common thoughts. Consequently, society did not value John Brown and he passed from this Earth a lonely and dejected man.

The tragedy is that we should have valued John Brown. He was an honest man, yet we were not honest with him. He was a kind man, yet we showed him no kindness. He was a just man, yet we gave him no justice. He was a compassionate man, yet we showed him no compassion. He was an intelligent man, yet we gave him no path upon which to explore and develop his intelligence. He was a loving man, yet we gave him no chance to share his love with us.

Yes, it is truly a tragedy that we do not value the John Browns of this world, as they are our only links to humanity. In our modern global culture of greed, dishonesty and false celebrity, there is little room for a decent, honest and kind man such as John Brown, and so, he is shunned and ignored. The women, who he so loved, would even ridicule him if they came into contact with him. These same women who had traded their precious femininity for money, possessions, power and position. In their quest to prove that they could do any man's job, and thus become as equally dishonest, callous and malicious as any man, they throw away the one thing that lifts them above this level to become the fairer sex. They know not what they lose.

In a world where it has become acceptable for politicians to lie and never be taken to account, for businesses to cheat and defraud their way in order to monopolise their particular trade, for many millions of individuals to shamelessly defraud benefit systems, for so called charities to be run unashamedly for profit, for honest morals to be publicly criticised, for education to be dumbed down to an alarming level, for gun cultures and drug cultures to be accepted as normal, for shallow celebrity to be worshipped and promoted above all else. In such a world as this, it is perhaps not surprising that there was little room for a fundamentally good man, the likes of John Brown.

For we undervalue the John Browns of this world without understanding their true worth. They are the direct link to humanity and, as humanity erodes, evil sweeps in, like a ferocious incoming tide, to fill the void. As humanity erodes, civilisation starts to collapse. Just as with the collapse of the Roman Empire, only, this time, due to the globalisation of greed, it will collapse globally. Yes, we undervalue the John Browns of this world at our peril.

Is it possible that we could halt or slow down the current trends and re-establish a better, more morally sound civilisation? Well, such an initiative will never come from an elected government or world leader of any description. But there is a chance, a very feint chance, that it might come from within the community. And if one community were able to turn the tables, others might follow, no matter how much they were resisted or penalised by those in authority. If we started to seek out the John Browns within our community and engage with them, talk with them, encourage them to talk to us, to share their knowledge, to share their goodness. Not for reward or recognition, but for the common good. John Brown would have responded to such an invitation with enthusiasm and love and, within a very short time, would be making a very positive contribution to his community. In his footsteps, others might follow. Others who had different latent aptitudes that they could develop for the common good. As the word spread, a wave of goodness might start to rise and seep throughout the community. We might yet return to a proper way of living. To morality. To humanity.

For each man is born with the light. The light of that precious jewel within his heart which, if burnished and cared for, can produce wondrous things. That so many allow this jewel to quickly become tarnished with corruption and greed, is the tragedy of our times. And each man is born with that spark which comes from the reservoir of life. A spark which knows no politics, no religion and no race, and yet which can, if nurtured, ignite our best instincts and illuminate the path of our existence.

For John Brown, his light has returned home now and his days are at an end. They were not worthless days, if only we had eyes to see the truth of them. Let us not be blind to the other John Browns who will come among us from time to time. Let us draw them into our hearts and learn from them. For there is much to learn on this Earth, and so few days in which to gather that understanding. Let us search in the recesses of our hearts to rekindle the light and burnish the jewel, that we might yet walk on the better path.

8. Verse

And so upon this path of life
We come into a place unknown
To witness all the toil and strife
Along this path we call our own

And in our hearts there burns a flame
That warms us in eternal hope
For when we turn our heads in shame
From duty we must ne'er elope

But walk the path that's straight and true
Through all the anger, noise and pain
And keep our faith in all we do
For ne'er we'll walk this path again

So be of good and open heart
And reach a hand to those that fall
For we must never drift apart
Let love and peace endure for all

And when we meet with hate or fear
Stand and let our light shine through
Become the rock for all held dear
That others there may witness too

And so inspire the love that burns
To hold us straight along the way
And cosset all that we might learn
Be thankful for each passing day

And let our children emulate
The ways we learned, the lines we drew
And never yet to hesitate
To let the flame of love burn true

Through every step and every test
But from that path to never stray
To let their conscience never rest
Be thankful for each passing day

For understanding is the key
To all the days that we accrue
Through all the tears and things that be
Do let your heart be always true

Walk with pride and firm of step
To help all those along the way
That they may come to learn, and yet
Be thankful for each passing day